OFFICE
DARES

CLASSIFIED

WARNING...WARNING...WARNING

You are not a daredevil. You may think you want to be one, but trust us, you'll come to your senses when you've lost your job. There's nothing wrong with being a couch daredevil, a person who dreams of doing wild and crazy things in their office to add some spice to their daily routine. That's OK. Just don't try any of the dares we describe in this book. Here's why: It's not fun losing your job. Remember ... you need your job. You have bills to pay. You need to eat, and you have that car payment every month. How are you going to manage to pay off that credit-card debt when you're collecting unemployment? You won't be able to.

So first, right up front, let's get this whole legal disclaimer thing out of the way. This is a humor book. The dares described in this book are for your READING pleasure. They are not meant to be tried, tested, implemented, or performed—not in any way, shape, or form. DO NOT DO ANY OF THESE DARES. You could damage property, get fired, or even get arrested. If you do not heed our warning, Cider Mill Press, the author, and everyone involved in the making of this book are not responsible for your actions. We do not condone, support, recommend, or suggest that anyone try, test, practice, or implement any of the dares, stunts, or schemes described herein. We are not responsible for your actions. Enjoy the book within your office or cubicle. Laugh out loud. Share it with your colleagues. Sure, you can say things to each other like, "Imagine what would happen if we did this ... or that ... in our office!" But leave it at that, and don't try these dares in real life.

Remember, you are not a daredevil. Repeat a few times before you turn this page: I AM NOT A DAREDEVIL.

If that doesn't get through to you, remember this:
YOU NEED YOUR JOB.

Glad we got that out of the way.

Now, let's have some fun. Read on!

The
UNDERGROUND MANUAL
of
OFFICE
DARES

By Lou Harry

CIDER MILL PRESS

BOOK
PUBLISHERS

Kennebunkport, Maine

13-Digit ISBN: 978-1-60433-055-7
10-Digit ISBN: 1-60433-055-4

This book may be ordered by mail from the publisher.
Please include $3.50 for postage and handling.
Please support your local bookseller first!

Books published by Cider Mill Press Book Publishers are available at special discounts for bulk purchases in the United States by corporations, institutions, and other organizations.
For more information, please contact the publisher.

Cider Mill Press Book Publishers
"Where good books are ready for press"
12 Port Farm Road
Kennebunkport, Maine 04046

Visit us on the Web!
www.cidermillpress.com

Design by Michael Rogalski
Typography: American Typewriter, Bookman, Capture it

Printed in China

1 2 3 4 5 6 7 8 9 0
First Edition

For Goldberg, Strunk, and Levy. Especially Levy.

Goldberg, maybe not so much.

Kidding. I'm just kidding. Goldberg was fine.

Oh, and Julie. And especially Pam. And her friends Mario and Luigi. (See, back in the day, Pam and I used to take long lunches and play *Super Mario Brothers* at her place.) (Nothing else happened. Stop snickering.)

I, Lou Harry, being of relatively sound mind and body—despite having spent a couple of decades in various workplaces—would like to thank my former bosses Budd Kalafski; Larry Graber; Kathy Kalafski; Herb and David Lipson; the aforementioned Goldberg, Strunk, and Levy; Betsy Kalish-Hendler; Ann Stack; Deborah Paul; and Todd Tobias. It couldn't have been easy for them, and I appreciate their hiring me. (In the case of two of them, I don't appreciate their firing me. But what can you do?)

I would like to express deep appreciation to Tambra and Paul White for their input. I'd also like to thank my family of inventive troublemakers, especially journalist-in-training Katherine Harry, for not only giving me the space to write but also providing valuable contributions to this manuscript. (Yes, they pulled the "tape the handle down on the kitchen-sink sprayer" stunt on me. And I fell for it. More than once.)

Special thanks to Robert and John Fields—two of the original office DAREDEVILS!

I would also like to acknowledge my publisher, John Whalen, who had the original idea for *Office Dares,* entrusted me with the project, and has the common sense to stay far, far away from any place I'm working. Because you never want to let your guard down.

Never.

INTRODUCTION

Dares get a bad rap. With good reason: They've gotten a lot of people in trouble. The essential characteristic of a dare is that it's something you wouldn't have done without prodding, without someone else putting your guts on the line. "I believe you do not have the spine to do this thing," implies the darer, and even the most self-aware of us are often tempted by—and sometimes succumb to—that deceptively innocent challenge.

While dares are most often associated with children and adolescents, dares can continue throughout one's life. "You don't have the guts" is a phrase that's been applied to everything from business investments to marriage commitments. In a neutral environment, the road of taking certain reckless actions may not be taken. But with the suggestion that you are less of a man (or woman) in someone else's eyes if you don't do it, you may go down that road.

That's all very abstract, of course. Dares are specific. Sometimes painfully or embarrassingly specific. But that's the fun of administering them. Those who administer dares have a touch of sadism in them. They have to; why else pressure someone to commit an act that has no possible financial or personal gain for either of the parties involved? This book is about a specific kind of dare: the office dare. The office has a number of key elements that make its dares unique.

1. *Office* implies job, implies a paycheck, implies added stakes. Whether your screwy behavior hurts the company's bottom line, or just ruins your reputation, the magnitude of the dare can impact the length of your employment. And everyone knows it.

2. *Office* also implies the expectation of a certain level of adult behavior. Why does this matter? Because dares are, for the most part, juvenile acts. That's the beauty of them. It's why we love them. Put them in the context of a workplace where grown-ups are expected to act like reasonable facsimiles of grown-ups, and you have significantly and gloriously magnified the chance of awkwardness.

3. The very act of administering or carrying out a dare in or around the office indicates that you are focusing on something besides what you are supposed to be doing, which is work. Any kind of downtime is suspect in most office environments. So when it comes to office dares, stealth is often a key factor. Don't ever let them see you scheme.

Putting these together leads to an obvious warning: You are the person who is ultimately responsible for what happens if you actually administer or execute any of the dares you will find in the following pages. Nobody's telling you to make the dare. Nobody's forcing the other party to carry out the dare.

You want to come looking for me? I dare you. On second thought, I don't. Just don't hold me responsible, OK?

Please?

HOW TO USE THIS BOOK

While the concept of the dare seems innate in the human species, there are still a few things you should know before diving into this book and attempting to inflict dares at your workplace.

Office Dares is divided into sections that correspond to certain aspects of office life. Each of these sections features a short introduction, followed by a list—sometimes a long list—of specific dares.

Need a dare to use in your cubicle? Head directly for that section. Want to challenge a co-worker to some elevator embarrassment? Well, I've got a section for you. There are also special sections mixed in between the chapters, including dares for the IT guys, special-day-at-the-office dares, and more.

If you've already flipped ahead, you may have noticed some strange coding after every dare listed. That's not the result of some typesetter losing his or her mind, nor is it evidence of the author of this book losing his mind. Instead, it's the result of a time-tested system for ranking dares. These ratings break down in the following way:

D	your standard **dare**
2D	the assertive **double dare**
2DD	the even more assertive **double-dog dare**
3D	the hackles-raising **triple dare**
3DD	the awe-inspiring **triple-dog dare**

Let's back up a second to explain. Anyone who ever spent time in a schoolyard knows that not all dares are created equal. There are *degrees* of daring.

The simplest is the *dare*. When someone dares you to do something, not doing it results in some loss of face. Then there's the *double dare* which, well, doubles the impact of that humiliation. The *double-dog dare* doubles that again. Now, the math may not make sense, but a *triple dare* is actually double a double-dog dare. And a *triple-dog dare* is about as daring as you can get.

As you go through this book and consider following through on the suggested dares, please pay close attention to the dare factor for each. Keep in mind that in many cultures, double-darers go first. Double-dare the wrong person, and you could end up ... well, turn the page, and you'll find lots of things you might be doing.

So let's get started. And good luck at the next salary review.

ELEVATOR DARES

To most people the elevator is merely a way of getting from point A (the lobby) to point B (your office). But for you, the darer, the smallest room in the building is also a place rife with possibilities for office challenges.

Whether you are too lazy to walk the stairs to your first-floor office, or a long-distance rider taking the vertical shuttle to the heights, here's a starter list of elevator dares to consider. But act quick: Your floor will be here in no time.

I DARE YOU	to push all the buttons while someone else is in the elevator with you. (D)
I DARE YOU	to push all the buttons while your boss is in the elevator with you. (2DD)
I DARE YOU	to walk into the elevator and stand facing the back wall for the entire ride. (D)
I DARE YOU	to hold onto the arm of the nearest co-worker when the elevator starts moving. (2D)
I DARE YOU	to, when you are the only person in the elevator, stand at the front and say, "Sorry, nope" each time the door opens and someone wants to get on. (2D)

I DARE YOU to sing "Free Falling" while riding on the elevator.
(D)

I DARE YOU to, every time you are in the elevator for an entire week, say to whoever is riding with you, "You know, I used to work as an elevator operator. Now there's a job that has its ups and downs."
(D)

I DARE YOU to make faces at the security camera on the elevator.
(D)

I DARE YOU to take your shoes off on the elevator.
(D)

Socks too.
(2D)

I DARE YOU	to make your floor selection on the elevator using your nose. **(D)**
I DARE YOU	to make your floor selection on the elevator using your toes. **(2DD)**
I DARE YOU	to shout "Hey, I wanted floor pi!" as the elevator moves between floors three and four. **(D)**
I DARE YOU	to, when the elevator stops on the 13th floor, in a very panicky voice say, "I wouldn't get off there if I were you." **(D)**
I DARE YOU	to take a blanket on the elevator and make a tent. **(2DD)**

I DARE YOU | to eat your lunch on the elevator.
(D)

I DARE YOU | to play solitaire on the floor of the elevator.
(2D)

I DARE YOU | and a friend to hold a limbo stick across the entrance to the elevator.
(2DD)

I DARE YOU | to hold the open button and not let go, no matter what anyone on the elevator says.
(2DD)

I DARE YOU | to add a pretend button to the top of the button grid that says "Wonkavator."
(D)

I DARE YOU | to hug everyone on the elevator.
(3D)

I DARE YOU | to call everyone on the elevator "Otis."
(D)

I DARE YOU | to decorate the elevator with photos of
your family.
(2D)

I DARE YOU | to decorate the elevator with photos of
your supervisor's family
(2DD).

IF IT'S A MIRRORED ELEVATOR,

I DARE YOU | to draw faces on the glass with lipstick.
(2D)

IF IT'S A MIRRORED ELEVATOR,

I DARE YOU	to write REDRUM on the glass in lipsick. (2DD)
I DARE YOU	to ask someone to give you a leg up so that you can reach the emergency door. (D)
I DARE YOU	to try to order a pizza through the elevator security phone. (D)
I DARE YOU	to ask to borrow a pen and then throw it out the next time the elevator door opens. (2D)
I DARE YOU	to ask to borrow a cell phone and then throw it out the next time the elevator door opens. (3DD)

CUBICLE
DARES

I f you are blessed with a workspace that includes four walls and a door, consider yourself lucky. But for many of us, an actual shut-the-door-and-leave-the-peons-out-there office just isn't a fact of work life. Instead, we've got those half-walls that subject us to the rambling personal phone calls made by our co-workers (and that let them listen to ours, the snoops). Looked at from above, we no doubt look like mice in some not-so-elaborate maze. And often we feel that way.

For the cubicle dwellers, here's a group of dares that can make the hours whiled away behind those half-walls at least a little more interesting.

I DARE YOU	to stage a puppet show over your cubicle wall. (D)
I DARE YOU	to raise the chairs of everyone in the office by one inch. (2D)
I DARE YOU	to raise the desk of a co-worker six inches off the ground, using bricks or other platforms under its feet. (2DD)
I DARE YOU	to decorate your cubicle with throw pillows. (D)
I DARE YOU	to decorate your cubicle with a bean-bag chair. (D)

PRIVELEGED
INFORMATION

I DARE YOU to do a day's work while seated in the bean-bag chair.
(2D)

I DARE YOU to not leave your chair for the entire day. Instead of getting up, you have to wheel around the office.
(2D)

I DARE YOU to glue a co-worker's office supplies to his or her desk.
(2D)

I DARE YOU to switch the desk drawers of two people in other cubicles.
(2D)

I DARE YOU to connect a "The Clapper" to a co-worker's computer monitor, and strategically clap throughout the day.
(2D)

I DARE YOU to call IT and ask where the "Any" key is.
(D)

I DARE YOU to call IT and ask them for help with a particularly challenging game of Minesweeper.
(D)

I DARE YOU to call IT and ask them for help clearing downloaded porn from your computer—even though there isn't any there.
(2D)

I DARE YOU to leave your cell phone in your desk drawer at the loudest possible ringer setting, leave the office, find another phone, and call your cell every five minutes for an hour.
(2D)

I DARE YOU to make a log cabin out of pencils on your desk.
(D)

I DARE YOU to keep a framed photo of the Baldwin brothers on your desk.
(D)

I DARE YOU to keep a framed photo of the Olympic beach volleyball team on your desk.
(D)

I DARE YOU to keep a framed photo of your boss's family on your desk.
(2DD)

I DARE YOU to use a permanent marker to paint all of your fingernails black.
(D)

I DARE YOU to write a letter using only correction fluid.
(D)

I DARE YOU to keep copies of the following on your desk: *The Communist Manifesto*, *Reba: My Story*, *The Sisterhood of the Traveling Pants*, a Portuguese-to-French dictionary, a baby-naming book, a Dora the Explorer coloring book, a guitar fake book, *Dianetics: The Modern Science of Mental Health*, *Sammy Spider's First Hanukkah*, an encyclopedia of psychological diseases, *Heart of Darkness*, and Dr. Seuss's *The 500 Hats of Bartholomew Cubbins*.
(2D)

I DARE YOU to make a 10-foot-long paper-clip chain.
(D)

I DARE YOU to jump rope with your 10-foot-long paper-clip chain.
(2D)

I DARE YOU to tie a sleeping co-worker's feet together using your 10-foot-long paper-clip chain. **(2DD)**

I DARE YOU to install a mini-basketball hoop, then repeatedly throw the ball over your wall into the neighboring cubicle, shouting "A little help!" each time. **(D)**

I DARE YOU to draw the outlines of feet on the floor of your cubicle, and practice dance steps every time you stand up. **(2D)**

I DARE YOU to wrap your office furniture in plastic slipcovers. **(D)**

I DARE YOU to fill a co-worker's desk drawers with packing peanuts. **(2D)**

I DARE YOU	to put empty liquor bottles in the drawer of a co-worker who just pulled an all-nighter. **(2DD)**
I DARE YOU	to put a live frog in the desk drawer of a co-worker. **(2DD)**
I DARE YOU	to bring a child who isn't yours to "Take Your Daughter to Work Day." **(3D).**
I DARE YOU	to write the words "Rake Me" in a co-worker's desktop Zen garden. **(D)**
I DARE YOU	to have yourself paged every hour on the hour. **(D)**

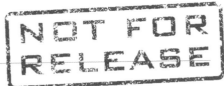

I DARE YOU to scream into your phone, "That will NOT do ... that will NOT do ... that will NOT do!"
(D)

I DARE YOU to make a chess board out of Post-Its on your wall.
(D)

I DARE YOU to replace light bulbs on the desks of key co-workers with black lights.
(D)

I DARE YOU to blow bubbles over your cubicle wall.
(D)

I DARE YOU to take at least three powers naps in a single day.
(2D)

I DARE YOU to install an alarm system for your cubicle.
(D)

I DARE YOU to dot your I's with little hearts on your next self-evaluation.
(2D)

I DARE YOU to write smileys randomly in your next self-evaluation.
(2DD)

I DARE YOU to set up an elaborate, domino-like display using office supplies, and call a meeting to demonstrate the fall-down.
(D)

I DARE YOU to string holiday lights and put up a tree in your cubicle ... in August.
(D)

| **I DARE YOU** | to set up an ant farm on your desk.
(D) |

| **I DARE YOU** | to get to second base (or allow someone to get to second base) at your cubicle—with a willing second party, of course.
(2D) |

| **I DARE YOU** | to get to third base (or allow someone to get to third base) at your cubicle—with a willing second party, of course.
(3D) |

| **I DARE YOU** | to go for a home run at your cubicle—with a willing second party, of course.
(3DD)
(Bonus: The dare-ee will earn the awe and respect of every reader of this book.) |

I DARE YOU to execute the Blast Out prank. Haven't heard of that one? Here's how it's done:

1. Turn off the power strip in a co-worker's cubicle.

2. Plug the cord for a portable radio into it.

3. Turn the radio to its highest volume.

4. Hide the radio behind his or her desk.

5. Go far, far away and wait until your co-worker comes into the office, is confused by the lack of power, realizes that the power strip is off, innocently turns it on, and gets blasted by the sound.

RESTRICTED

PRIVATE OFFICE DARES

If you've been lucky, talented, or duplicitous enough to land in your own four-walled office space, bully for you. Just know that with that ability to close your door or see out a window comes a new set of dares. Proceed with caution, lest you find yourself back in a cubicle.

And remember that those cubicle dwellers outside your walls have already deemed you a target for pranks, just by virtue of your ability to shut them out. Be warned.

Note: Whenever it's obvious, the dare implies that your office has windows and that there are no obstructions keeping you from being seen from at least part of a common area. Where would the fun be otherwise?

I DARE YOU to get on the office intercom just after the start of the workday and ask everyone to please stand for the Pledge of Allegiance—and then recite the Pledge of Allegiance.
(2D)

I DARE YOU to play handball in your office.
(2D)

I DARE YOU to affix glow-in-the-dark stars to your office ceiling.
(D)

I DARE YOU to mush your face against the glass when a co-worker walks by.
(D)

I DARE YOU to mush your face against the glass when your supervisor walks by.
(2D)

I DARE YOU to mush your face against the glass when a member of the media walks by.
(2DD)

I DARE YOU to watch a full season of a TV series on DVD in a week.
(2D)

I DARE YOU to do a handstand in your office.
(D)

I DARE YOU to do a handstand on your desk.
(2D)

I DARE YOU to do a forward roll in your office.
(D)

I DARE YOU to stand on your desk and do the Charleston.
(2DD)

I DARE YOU | to keep your shirt off for a half an hour while in your office.
(3D)

I DARE YOU | to get down on your knees and pray three times a day.
(D)

I DARE YOU | to get down on your knees and kick your feet like a donkey three times a day.
(2D)

I DARE YOU | to build a house of cards on your desk at least four stories tall.
(D)

I DARE YOU | to string a tin-can phone between your office and the next.
(D)

I DARE YOU | to cook a hamburger for lunch on a George Foreman Grill in your office.
(2D)

I DARE YOU | to frame your high-school essay contest certificate, perfect-attendance bowling league award, or some other worthless document you've won, and hang it in your office.
(D)

I DARE YOU | to offer some beef jerky to the next person who comes into your office.
(D)

I DARE YOU | to offer a massage to the next person who comes into your office.
(2DD)

IF IT ISN'T ALREADY THERE,

I DARE YOU to put your name and title on your office door with press-on letters.
(D)

IF IT ISN'T ALREADY THERE,

I DARE YOU to paint your name on your door.
(3D)

I DARE YOU to hang a beaded curtain at the entrance to your office.
(2D)

I DARE YOU to put a tip jar on your desk.
(D)

I DARE YOU to use a tape measure to compare the dimensions of your co-workers' offices to yours.
(2D)

I DARE YOU to set up a waiting area outside your office, complete with chairs and old magazines.
(2D)

I DARE YOU to list a co-worker's private office in the real estate section of the local paper as available for subletting.
(D)

COMMON AREA DARES

No space at the office truly belongs to the worker. Yes, your office or cubicle at least feels like it's yours. Kind of. But there's a whole lot of space between your territory and that of your co-workers. In that theoretical neutral zone, a whole lot can happen. There, dares are more public, risks are greater, and the possibilities are infinite.

Of course, if I listed all of those infinite possibilities, this would be an impossibly heavy book. So I've limited myself to the following.

I DARE YOU | to give yourself a thin moustache using a permanent marker.
(2D; 3D if you are a woman)

I DARE YOU | to fake a major paper-cut.
(2D)

I DARE YOU | to post "wet paint" signs randomly around the office.
(D)

I DARE YOU | to stay after hours and transform an office bulletin board into an elementary-school-style presentation on the importance of good oral hygiene.
(D)

I DARE YOU | to drop and do twenty.
(D)

I DARE YOU | to break the points off of every pencil in the office.
(DD)

I DARE YOU | to select a co-worker and repeat the last word he or she says in every conversation with you.
(D)

I DARE YOU | to make a trail from the break room to the restroom using the shavings from office pencil-sharpeners.
(D)

I DARE YOU | to tell a superior that his fly is undone even though it isn't.
(2D)

I DARE YOU | to clandestinely "borrow" a co-worker's cell phone, set the ringer volume on high, and hide it in another person's desk.
(2D)

I DARE YOU | to clandestinely "borrow" a co-worker's cell phone, set the ringer volume on high, and hide it in the office refrigerator.
(2D)

I DARE YOU | to clandestinely "borrow" a co-worker's cell phone, set the ringer volume on high, and hide it above a panel of the drop ceiling.
(2D)

I DARE YOU | to clandestinely "borrow" a co-worker's cell phone, set the ringer volume on high, and hide it in your boss's office.
(2D)

I DARE YOU to pick up a stack of folders and walk around the office nonstop for 45 minutes, pretending you are doing something important.
(D)

I DARE YOU to climb into the office ductwork.
(2DD)

I DARE YOU to bicycle to your cubicle or office.
(2D)

I DARE YOU to skateboard to your cubicle or office.
(2D)

I DARE YOU to hurdle a series of office chairs set up along an office corridor.
(2DD)

I DARE YOU | to wear wheeled shoes to work and glide around the office on them all day.
(2D)

I DARE YOU | to ask, within earshot of a number of co-workers, if anyone would be willing to switch clothes with you for the day.
(2D)

I DARE YOU | to make a coffee-cup pyramid with at least a six-coffee-cup base.
(D)

I DARE YOU | to make a wastebasket pyramid with at least a six-wastebasket base.
(D)

I DARE YOU | to make a desk pyramid with at least a six-desk base.
(3DD)

I DARE YOU | to hold the door open for the people behind you ... and keep holding the door open for minutes even though nobody is behind them.
(D)

I DARE YOU | to stand outside your office parking lot with a sign that reads "Valet."
(D)

I DARE YOU | to fax, from somewhere off-site, a cover sheet noting that the following is a document "of vital importance" to your boss—with no further pages.
(2D)

I DARE YOU | to stand outside your office parking lot with a sign that reads "Will work for food."
(2D)

I DARE YOU | to stand outside your office parking lot with a sign that reads "Soon to be jobless."
(3D)

I DARE YOU | to recreate, to the best of your ability, your boss's resume, print it, and leave a copy in every copying machine in the office.
(2D)

I DARE YOU | to recreate, to the best of your ability, your boss's resume, print it, and send a copy to your top competitors.
(3DD)

I DARE YOU | to skip in the office.
(D)

I DARE YOU | to gallop in the office.
(D)

| I DARE YOU | to walk on your hands in the office. (D) |

| I DARE YOU | to walk with a book on your head in the office. (D) |

| I DARE YOU | to trip twice in the same office corridor. (D) |

| I DARE YOU | to resort, incorrectly, the office mail. (D) |

| I DARE YOU | to put a pair of shoes in each of your co-workers' mail slots. (D) |

| I DARE YOU | to put an egg-salad sandwich in each of your co-workers' mail slots. (2D) |

I DARE YOU to fake a mild case of Tourette's syndrome.
(2DD)

I DARE YOU to fake a major case of Tourette's syndrome.
(3DD)

I DARE YOU to make a snow angel outside of your office building.
(2D)

FURTHER

I DARE YOU to complain to the boss that the snow angel in front of the building (the one you made) is a blatant religious symbol and an attempt to identify one religion as the correct one and, thus, is a violation of your constitutional rights.
(2DD)

I DARE YOU to pull off the Tidal Wave prank. Aren't familiar with that one? Here's how it goes:

1. Find 10 or so plastic cups.

2. Staple them together in a row.

3. Put them in a conspicuous place.

4. Fill them with water.

5. Wait for some poor fool to come by and, trying to be helpful, pick one up. The rest will come along for the ride and spill all over the place.

CONFERENCE ROOM DARES

I n some workplaces, the conference room is the de facto dining hall. In some, the conference room is just a waste of space. In others, it's the place where important—or, at least, larger—meetings are held.

These dares, for the most part, apply to the latter type. When attention is focused, there are dares to be had. Of course, if your office is small enough that key meetings happen in your supervisor's office, in a common area, or elsewhere in the building, adjust accordingly.

I DARE YOU to take a Hannah Montana notebook into the next staff meeting.
(D)

I DARE YOU to use the phrase "Right on!" after a supervisor's statement.
(D)

I DARE YOU to ask "Could you repeat that last part?" four times during a supervisor's presentation.
(2DD)

I DARE YOU to switch seats in the middle of a supervisor's presentation without any explanation.
(D)

I DARE YOU to switch seats twice during a supervisor's presentation without any explanation.
(2D)

I DARE YOU | to bring a large cushion into the conference room and sit on it during a meeting.
(D)

I DARE YOU | to place a whoopee cushion on a co-worker's seat prior to a meeting.
(2D)

I DARE YOU | to put an egg-salad sandwich on a co-worker's seat prior to a meeting.
(2DD)

I DARE YOU | to shine a flashlight on the screen during an audio-visual presentation.
(2D)

I DARE YOU | to play table hockey with the conference-room drink coasters.
(D)

I DARE YOU to play footsie with someone on the other side of the table. (If yours is a particularly wide conference table, then I dare you to play footsie with the person sitting next to you.
(2D)

IF A DECISION MUST BE MADE,

I DARE YOU to suggest it should be made through the Rock Paper Scissors method.
(D)

I DARE YOU to, after a presentation, send your boss a review of the presenter's performance.
(2DD)

I DARE YOU to interrupt a presentation at least 10 minutes into it and ask the presenter to please start again.
(2DD)

I DARE YOU to, when the lights are turned off for a video presentation, state that it makes you uncomfortable and request that they be turned back on.
(2D)

I DARE YOU to interrupt a presentation at least 10 minutes into it and ask that the presenter move things along.
(3D)

I DARE YOU to pop bubble wrap during a meeting.
(2D)

I DARE YOU to do a spit take during a meeting.
(2DD)
(FYI: In the comedy business, a spit take is the moment when you've taken a mouthful of a drink, hear something shocking, and then spontaneously spit out the beverage.)

I DARE YOU to use the computer in the conference room to watch *SpongeBob SquarePants*.
(D)

I DARE YOU to use the computer in the conference room to watch "adult material" on the wide-screen TV.
(3DD)

[CONFIDENTIAL]

COPY
MACHINE
DARES

Back in the days of mimeographed copies, dare options were more limited. Sure, you could dare someone to do some heavy huffing of the ink, but that was about it. (If you are under 30, you probably have no idea what I'm talking about.)

The invention of the now-ubiquitous photocopying machine changed all of that. Now, with the pushing of a few buttons, a whole universe of daring possibilities arise. And all it costs the company is a little ink and paper.

Here's a starter list. Just don't let a copy fall into the wrong hands, lest suspicions arise.

I DARE YOU | to use the office copy machine to take a photo of your face.
(D)

I DARE YOU | to use the office copy machine to take a photo of your butt.
(2D)

I DARE YOU | to use the office copy machine to take a photo of someone else's butt.
(2DD)

I DARE YOU | to post any of your butt copies in a prominent place in the office.
(2D)

I DARE YOU | to use your butt copy as your screen saver.
(2DD)

I DARE YOU to use your butt copy as someone else's screen saver.
(3D)

I DARE YOU to use the office copy machine to make copies of your management team's photos, shrink them, and make finger puppets out of them.
(D)

I DARE YOU to use the office copy machine to take a photo of a small animal. (May I suggest a ferret?)
(2D)

I DARE YOU to make a copy of a copy of a copy of a copy, etc., shrinking the copy down by 5 percent every time.
(D)
(Frankly, I don't have the math brain to picture what this would end up looking like, so if you happen to do it and find out, please let me know.)

I DARE YOU to reproduce campaign posters on the office copy machine, and drop hints that you are running for Congress.
(2D)

I DARE YOU to make a fake I.D. using your office copy machine.
(D)

I DARE YOU to cut out and switch the captions on two cartoons from *The New Yorker*, copy them so that the cut is invisible, and post them prominently with a note saying "Hilarious."
(D)

I DARE YOU to make enough copies of a *New York Times* crossword puzzle for the entire rank-and-file staff, and distribute them via interoffice mail with a faked note from your boss on each, saying, "Due in my office by 3 P.M. No exceptions."
(2DD)

RESTROOM DARES

When you gotta go, you gotta go. And when you go into the office restroom, you'll not only find what you need to take care of your needs, you'll also find a whole new world of dare options. Plus some privacy to carry them out.

Knowing that there's a high risk of unpleasantness in this particular room, I've tried to avoid the gross dares and pranks you learned at your summer camp or college fraternity. You're more creative than that, aren't you? (OK, so I couldn't resist one or two.)

So, no need to raise your hand. Just head to the head, and consider these restroom dares, specially selected to leave your co-workers flushed.

I DARE YOU to strip down to a swimsuit and sponge-bathe yourself.
(3D)

I DARE YOU to take a strand of toilet paper and see how far you can pull it out the door and down the hall without breaking it.
(2DD)

I DARE YOU to leave an unwrapped Milky Way bar in a water-filled sink.
(D)

I DARE YOU to carry an entire Sunday edition of the *New York Times* into the restroom and read it while on the toilet.
(2D)

I DARE YOU to take one of those fart-making toys into the restroom and have at it.
(D)

I DARE YOU to leave a dish of tampons on the men's room counter.
(2D)

I DARE YOU to loudly sing all of "My Favorite Things" while sitting in a restroom stall.
(2D)

I DARE YOU to loudly sing a sea chantey while sitting in a restroom stall.
(A suggestion: "Barrett's Privateers," a very catchy tune by Canadian singer-songwriter Stan Rogers)
(2D)

I DARE YOU to shut off the lights in the restroom every chance you get throughout an entire day—when co-workers are in the stalls, of course.
(2D)

I DARE YOU | to leave a newspaper in a restroom stall with the most provocative personal ads circled.
(D)

I DARE YOU | to see if the baby-changing station attached to the wall can hold you.
(2D)

I DARE YOU | to pull the ever-popular Saran-Wrapped Toilet Seat prank.
(3D)
(If you have to ask what this is, well, you're better off not knowing. Just keep moving along. Nothing to see here.)

I DARE YOU | to install an eye chart inside the handicapped stall.
(D)

| **I DARE YOU** | to do any gymnastic move using the hand rails in the handicapped stall. **(D)** |

| **I DARE YOU** | to, while sitting on a toilet, call "Hot Potato!" and throw your underwear into the next stall. **(2DD)** |

| **I DARE YOU** | to bring cleaning supplies to the office and, without explanation, clean the restroom yourself. **(2D)** |

| **I DARE YOU** | to put origami folds in the toilet paper every time you finish up in the bathroom. (See instructions on next page) **(D)** |

CLASSIFIED

INFORMATION

Here's how to do it:

1. First, make sure that the toilet paper comes over the top of the roll, not under the bottom. (If it comes under the bottom, you're s--- out of luck.)

2. Fold the point of the bottom-left corner (your left, not the TP's left) up to the upper right, so that what was the bottom of the roll now lines up with what was the left side.

3. Take what is now the bottom point and fold it so that what was just the left side is now the top. It should now look like a triangle is emerging from the roll.

4. Flip the triangle so that it is now pointed up

5. Fold the new bottom left and right corners under, so that the final design looks like an on-its-point square emerging from the roll. If your company logo is a simple one, draw it here.

COMPUTER DARES

What did the office darer do 25 years
ago when the office computer, if there
was one, was about the size of a
refrigerator and parked somewhere in the
company's nether regions? How did drones
while away the hours without solitaire?
Without Free Cell? Without the ability to
Google ex-boyfriends and -girlfriends? More
importantly—and more relevant to this book:
What did office darers do without the
personal computer?

But I suppose there's no need to worry about
those barbaric days. Today, with a PC on
nearly every desk, opportunities for "daring-
do" have multiplied.

Here are some to get you started. And,
remember, thanks to your computer, you can
always do an Internet search for more. You
never know what you might find.

I DARE YOU | e-mail around the office a bracketed betting pool for the Little League playoffs and World Series.
(2D)

I DARE YOU | to Google your boss's name and "bastard."
(D)

I DARE YOU | to find someone somewhere in the country with the same name as you and start copying that person on all of your e-mail.
(D)

I DARE YOU | to e-mail everyone in the company announcing that you are starting a book club—and then, once people have signed up, announce that the first book is *Night School Nurses*.
(2DD)

I DARE YOU to send an e-mail to your boss from someone else's computer.
(2D)

I DARE YOU to send an e-mail from your boss's computer.
(2DD)

I DARE YOU to send an e-mail from your boss's computer announcing that the office will close at 3 P.M. today.
(3D)

I DARE YOU to send an e-mail from your boss's computer announcing an across-the-board, five-percent pay raise.
(3DD)

I DARE YOU to use a photo of your boss as a screen saver.
(D)

I DARE YOU	to do your income taxes on your office computer. (D)
I DARE YOU	to send all your e-mails for the day cc'd to **Bob@abbafanclub.org**. (2D)
I DARE YOU	to brag, in the middle of the afternoon, about how well you are doing in an online poker tournament. (2D)
I DARE YOU	to fit 200 games of computer solitaire into a single workday. (D)
I DARE YOU	to send a memo to the CFO extolling the value of converting the office to wind power. (D)

I DARE YOU to create MySpace or Facebook accounts for everyone in your office.
(2D)

I DARE YOU to sell office supplies on Ebay.
(2DD)

I DARE YOU to respond to an e-mailed request to purchase school fundraising products (such as wrapping paper or tins of popcorn) from a co-worker's child by sending back a note saying "Sorry, I don't like kids."
(2D)

I DARE YOU to send a note to the entire company asking that whoever took your Sea World snow globe kindly return it.
(2D)

| **I DARE YOU** | to MapQuest the distance between your office and every fast-food franchise in the area, and post the information. (D) |

| **I DARE YOU** | to MapQuest the distance between your office and every strip club and adult bookstore in the area, and post the information. (2D |

This document is for use by the intended recipient and contains information that is privileged or confidential.

BREAK
ROOM
DARES

Where do you go when you aren't doing what you get paid to do? The break room, of course—that special place that is home to the water cooler, the coffee machine, and that guy from accounting who never seems to be at his desk. It's the place where things no one wants are dumped for the taking, and where sign-up sheets for co-workers' kids' school, scout and youth-group fundraisers attempt to guilt you into grossly overpaying for items you don't want.

(Note: In some offices, the break room and the kitchenette are one and the same. Since there are plenty of dares for both, I chose to split them into separate sections. If you've got an issue with that, by all means send me a memo.)

In large part because of its nature as a cross-departmental congregating point, the break room is also a great place for office dares. Consider these.

I DARE YOU to take items off the desks of absent co-workers, arrange them on the table in the office break room, apply price tags, set up an honor box, and post a sign saying "Office Charity Garage Sale, Today Only."
(3DD)

I DARE YOU to set up a hallway bowling alley using the break room's empty water jugs.
(D)

I DARE YOU to write "Contaminated" on a full water jug.
(D)

I DARE YOU to fill the water-cooler with Kool-Aid.
(2D)

I DARE YOU	to fill the water-cooler with Kool-Aid, and draw an outline on the wall of the Kool-Aid guy as if he just burst through the wall. (2DD)
I DARE YOU	to create "dribble cups" by pricking holes into random cups in the water-cooler stack. (D)
I DARE YOU	to drink grape juice from a wine bottle in the break room. (2D)
I DARE YOU	to drink wine from a grape-juice bottle in the break room. (2DD)
I DARE YOU	to fill the candy machine's coin-return area with buttons. (D)

I DARE YOU | to tell whoever made the brownies that they really weren't very good.
(2DD; 2D if they actually weren't very good.)

I DARE YOU | to bribe the snack-delivery guy into letting you put personal items belonging to a co-worker into one of the corkscrew slots of the candy machine.
(3D)

I DARE YOU | to leave a note for the snack-machine refill guy saying that there will be consequences if he doesn't start stocking Rollos.
(D)

YOU KNOW THAT AREA AT THE BOTTOM OF THE SNACK MACHINE WHERE THE SNACKS DROP AFTER THEY ARE PURCHASED?

I DARE YOU | to fill that area with shaving cream.
(2DD)

I DARE YOU to make coffee-filter suns and decorate the break room with them.
(2D)

I DARE YOU to wear a coffee filter on your head.
(2D)

I DARE YOU to write fortune-cookie-like sayings on a few-dozen sugar packets.
(D)

I DARE YOU to replace the coffee your office usually drinks with Folgers Crystals.
(D)

I DARE YOU to mix a box of feminine pads in with the coffee packets.
(D)

CONFIDENTIAL

I DARE YOU to cover the entrance of the break room with yellow "Caution" tape.
(D)

I DARE YOU to draw a chalk outline of a body in the break room.
(D)

I DARE YOU to draw a chalk outline of a chicken in the break room.
(2D)

I DARE YOU to climb on top of the candy machine and toss fun-sized Milky Ways at anyone who comes near you.
(3D)

I DARE YOU to place tablecloths and candles on the tables, turn off the fluorescent lights, and play the violin during your lunch hour.
(2D)

IF YOUR BREAK ROOM HAS A TELEVISION SET,

I DARE YOU | to argue loudly for the plaintiff on whatever *Judge Judy/People's Court*-type show happens to be on.
(2D)

IF YOUR BREAK ROOM HAS A TELEVISION SET,

I DARE YOU | to walk in and change the channels whenever you see that someone else is watching.
(2DD)

I DARE YOU | to bring a hot plate to the office and set up a made-to-order omelet station in the break room.
(3D)

I DARE YOU | to declare that you have a peanut allergy and insist that all Snickers candy bars be removed from the vending machines.
(2D)

I DARE YOU | to drink all of the non-dairy creamers and leave the empties on the table.
(D)

I DARE YOU | to set up a game of Chutes and Ladders in the break room and challenge all comers.
(2D)

I DARE YOU | to fill out the entire Girl Scout cookie order form with fictional orders.
(2D)

I DARE YOU | to, when the Girl Scout cookies are finally delivered, weasel at least one cookie from everyone who actually ordered and paid for them.
(2D)

I DARE YOU | to try to return the unused portion of a half-eaten fundraiser candy bar.
(2D)

OFFICE REFRIGERATOR & KITCHENETTE DARES

S tocked with frozen dinners and sad leftovers, sodas destined to be stolen, and the remains of yesterday's meeting in the conference room, the office refrigerator is sometimes a part of the break room. Sometimes not. By virtue of the large number of dares that can be applied to its contents, though, I'm giving it its own section.

If you've got a problem with that, I dare you to do something about it. On second thought, I don't. We're cool, right?

Now, where were we? Oh, yes. Dine carefully as you consider these dares.

I DARE YOU to open all of the frozen lunches in the office freezer and swap the entrees into different boxes.
(2D)

I DARE YOU to write your name on all the unlabeled items in the refrigerator.
(2DD)

I DARE YOU to write your boss's name on all the unlabeled items in the refrigerator.
(2DD)

I DARE YOU to cross off the names on all the labeled items in the refrigerator.
(2D)

I DARE YOU to cross off the names on all the labeled items in the refrigerator and replace each with the name of the last person from the company who was fired or laid off.
(2D)

I DARE YOU	to insert inspiring messages on slips of paper into the refrigerated bag-lunches. (A suggestion: "Have the greatest day of your life!") **(D)**

I DARE YOU	to insert uninspiring messages into the refrigerated bag-lunches. (A suggestion: "Boy, it sucks to be a drone, doesn't it?") **(2D)**

I DARE YOU	to insert secret-admirer notes into the refrigerated bag-lunches. **(2D)**

I DARE YOU	to swap food items in the refrigerated bag-lunches. **(2D)**

| **I DARE YOU** | to, just before your office's busiest lunch period, set the microwave on 59 minutes (or its highest time setting) and hit START.
(D) |

| **I DARE YOU** | to, while other people are waiting in line for the microwave, taste what you've just cooked, say "Another minute," put it back in, and repeat this sequence at least three times.
(2D) |

| **I DARE YOU** | to, when someone with food in the microwave leaves the kitchen area for whatever reason, take out their entrée, have a bite, and put the rest back where it was.
(2DD) |

I DARE YOU to, when someone with food in the microwave leaves the kitchen area for whatever reason, take out their entrée and hide it.
(2D)

I DARE YOU put a fake bloody finger in the ice-cube maker.
(2D)

I DARE YOU to put tampons in the cheese drawer.
(2D)

I DARE YOU to bring a blender to the office and make a beverage out of all the unclaimed items in the refrigerator.
(2D)

FURTHER

I DARE YOU to drink it.
(3DD)

| **I DARE YOU** | to put an unpackaged and unwrapped roasted turkey leg in the office refrigerator.
(D) |

| **I DARE YOU,** | to gnaw on a tube of raw cookie dough during a break.
(D) |

| **I DARE YOU** | to fill the office refrigerator with frozen turkeys.
(D) |

| **I DARE YOU** | to put a six-pack of beer in the office refrigerator.
(D) |

| **I DARE YOU** | to put a six-pack of beer labeled with a co-worker's name in the office refrigerator.
(2D) |

I DARE YOU to put a six-pack of beer—minus one beer—in the office refrigerator.
(2D)

I DARE YOU to put a mini-keg in the office refrigerator with a note saying "Help yourself."
(2DD)

I DARE YOU to put all of the personal objects from a co-worker's desk onto the top shelf of the refrigerator.
(2DD)

I DARE YOU to insert unexpected food items into refrigerated sandwiches.
(2DD)

LUNCH BREAK DARES

t's halfway through the day. Time for a bite to eat. For some, lunch just means a trip to the break room or office cafeteria. (See Break Room Dares, elsewhere in this book, if you are one of those can't-leave-the-premises folks). For others, lunch means getting away from the office—often as far away as possible.

Still, being outside the company walls doesn't mean you have to be away from office dares. Far from it. The outside world offers a new batch of dares to sample. Just make sure you get back to the office before someone ... you know ... gets in trouble.

I DARE YOU | to invite the boss out for lunch and take him or her to White Castle.
(D)

I DARE YOU | to invite the boss out for lunch, take him or her to White Castle, and wait for him or her to pay.
(2D)

I DARE YOU | to call "shotgun" and run around the passenger side when going out to eat with your boss and others.
(D)

WHEN LUNCHING WITH THE BOSS ON THE COMPANY DIME,

I DARE YOU | to ask the waiter or waitress, "Hmmm, now what's the most expensive thing on the menu?"
(D)

CONFIDENTIAL

WHEN DINING WITH A GROUP OF CO-WORKERS,

I DARE YOU | to unscrew the lid of the salt/pepper/oregano/whatever-condiment-is-on-the-table shaker and set the lid on top, so that when it is shaken the lid falls off and everything pours out.
(2D)

I DARE YOU | to blame your co-worker after pulling the above "unscrew the lid" trick.
(2DD)

I DARE YOU | to blame your supervisor after pulling the above "unscrew the lid" trick.
(3D)

I DARE YOU | to tell your co-worker, after the check arrives, how honored you are that he or she took you to lunch for no particular reason, and that you'd be happy to pay the tip.
(2D)

I DARE YOU to take a co-worker to lunch at a "gentleman's club."

(**2D**; **2DD** if you are a woman and the co-worker is a man; **3DD** if you are a man and the co-worker is a woman)

I DARE YOU to take lunch orders for a local eatery from a group of co-workers, head out of the office, then take the afternoon off.
(**2D**)

I DARE YOU to, while dining out, order everything on the left side of the menu (with a nod to the classic movie *Diner*).
(**D**)

I DARE YOU to, after ordering everything on the left side of the menu, actually eat everything on the left side of the menu.
(**D**)

I DARE YOU | to challenge a supervisor to a hot-dog-eating contest.
(D)

I DARE YOU | to, when the boss is in the restaurant restroom, add salt to his or her drink.
(2D)

WHEN LUNCHING WITH YOUR BOSS,

I DARE YOU | to put ketchup on your steak.
(D)

WHEN LUNCHING WITH YOUR BOSS,

I DARE YOU | to put ketchup on *his* steak.
(2D)

I DARE YOU | to order 12 pizzas under your boss's name and have them delivered to the office.
(2D)

I DARE YOU to stand at the office entrance and write down the time people leave for lunch and the time they return. And post the results.
(2D)

I DARE YOU to pretend for two weeks that you are going to a gym during your lunch hour.
(D)

I DARE YOU to, while out at lunch, leave a note on a co-worker's car saying "Sorry about the dent" and not leaving a name.
(D) (Of course, you should disguise your handwriting.)

I DARE YOU to eat six Arby's Big Beef and Cheddar sandwiches.
(2D)

I DARE YOU to eat a dozen White Castle burgers.
(2D)

I DARE YOU to back into a fast-food drive-thru while co-workers are riding in your car.
(2D)

BULLETIN BOARD DARES

Dares that make use of office bulletin boards aren't the gutsiest dares in the world—primarily because the dare-ee isn't usually around when they are read.

Still, daring someone to post something awkward or embarrassing has its pleasures. Plus, most of them entail the dramatic moment that occurs when someone catches on and tears the thing down. Consider some of these.

I DARE YOU	to post notice that you will offer a big wet kiss to anyone who loses 12 pounds. **(2DD)**
I DARE YOU	to follow through with the above if someone does, in fact, lose 12 pounds. **(2DD)**
I DARE YOU	to post notice of a $5 reward for anyone who finds your pet ferret. **(D)**
I DARE YOU	to post notice of a $5 reward for anyone who can find you a date by Friday. **(2D)**
I DARE YOU	to post notice of a $5 reward for anyone who can find a date for your pet ferret by Friday. **(2DD)**

I DARE YOU	to use a yellow highlighter on random words on the posted OSHA notice. **(2D)**
I DARE YOU	to use a yellow highlighter on words on the posted OSHA notice in such a way that a "hidden message" is revealed. **(2DD)**
I DARE YOU	to use correction fluid to cover up innocuous words in a posted bulletin, thus making it look as if provocative parts have been censored. **(2D)**
I DARE YOU	to use a computer translation program to translate the latest company memo into Japanese and back again, then post the results in a prominent place in the office. **(D)**

HIGHLY RESTRICTED

I DARE YOU | to post a petition demanding that a bidet be installed in the company restrooms "in the interest of international relations."
(D)

I DARE YOU | to spell out the boss's name on the bulletin board using Fruit Roll-Ups.
(2D)

FURTHER,

I DARE YOU, | at the end of the day, to eat those same Fruit Roll-Ups.
(2DD)

I DARE YOU | to add a letter to the motivational poster so that it says: "There is no I in Teaim."
(2D)

VERBAL DARES

hat you say and how you say it can be as daring as what you do.

And while some of the other dare categories in this book contain verbal dares, it seemed sensible to segregate a sample of them into their own chapter.

Here's a set of office dares designed to tilt the ears of even the most keep-to-herself staffer.

I DARE YOU to spend a day only speaking in quotes from *The Office*.
(D)

I DARE YOU to walk through the office absent-mindedly singing the *Barney* theme song. ("I love you, you love me ...")
(D)

I DARE YOU to, in the middle of a conversation, declare "Dance break!" and do your best moves.
(2D)

I DARE YOU to respond to "Good morning" with "Nope."
(D)

I DARE YOU to, instead of saying "Good morning," say "Good morning, America."
(D)

I DARE YOU | to, instead of saying "Good morning," sing "Good morning, America, how are you …" and as much of the rest of the song "City of New Orleans" as you can remember.
(D)

I DARE YOU | to, instead of saying "Good morning," sing "Good morning, starshine, the earth says hello …" (or as much of that song from the musical *Hair* as you can remember).
(D)

I DARE YOU | to announce loudly—and for no reason—that it is 2:42.
(D)

FURTHER

I DARE YOU | to announce loudly—also for no reason—that it is 2:47.
(2D)

I DARE YOU | to count the times the youngest person in your office says "like" in a single day.
(D)

I DARE YOU | to memorize two paragraphs from a newspaper op-ed piece and work them into today's conversation.
(2D)

I DARE YOU | to memorize three lines from a *Cathy* comic strip and work them into today's conversation.
(2D)

I DARE YOU | to work the following word or words into a workday conversation:

réchauffé (definition: warmed up or rehashed)
(D)

jactancy (boasting)
(D)

facinorous (wicked)
(D)

Islets of Langerhans (a group of endocrine cells in the pancreas)
(D)

defenestrate (to throw out through a window)
(D)

Charo (a questionably talented singer-dancer)
(D)

Manny Mota (one of the greatest-named players in baseball history)
(D)

physiatrist (not sure what that means, look it up—that's why you have a computer at your desk)
(D)

ascertain (to figure out from available information)
(D)

I DARE YOU to work the following sentence into an office conversation:

"Try as I might, I can't seem to cure these hemorrhoids."
(2D)

"Paris Hilton. Now there's an actress."
(D)

"*Catwoman* was much better than *The Dark Knight*."
(D)

"I prefer the X-Men style of management."
(D)

"That's not what they said on *Entertainment Tonight*."
(D)

"If I hear the phrase 'out of the box' one more time, I'm going to throw an Aeron chair out the window."
(D)

"If I hear the phrase 'out of the box' one more time, I'm going to defenestrate an Aeron chair."
(DD)

"I wish I'd worn underwear today."
(D)

"You know, there is actually a house in New Orleans that they call the Rising Sun."
(D)

RECEPTIONIST DARES

I realize I'm offering a lot of wild dares in this book. But one thing I won't do is recommend or even suggest any dare that impacts on a receptionist.

You can mess with the mind of a CEO. You can execute a prank on a CFO. You can do what you will with the dudes on the loading dock. But whatever you do, never ever, ever make life any more difficult for the receptionist than it already is.

Now, onward.

INTERN DARES

They are a special breed, the interns. Unlike seemingly everyone else in the office, they are on the premises to learn, not just collect a paycheck. They actually aspire to be in your position—which is kind of disturbing, but nonetheless it's the way things are.

Given the intern's unique combination of earnestness and neediness, he or she is a prime candidate to be the subject of dares. It would be a shame to let such innocence and gullibility go to waste.

Of course, as with the rest of the dares in this book, I suggest that the darer carefully consider the potential professional and legal fallout from any of these being traced to you. And feel free, if you are so inclined, to consider the long-term psychological impact of your actions on an impressionable mind.

But that kind of ruins the fun.

I DARE YOU | to tell the new intern wrong names for half the staff.
(2D)

I DARE YOU | to tell the new intern that the boss likes it when you ask lots and lots of questions ... about flowers.
(D)

I DARE YOU | to tell the new intern that the boss likes it when you ask lots and lots of questions ... about dinosaurs.
(D)

I DARE YOU | to tell the new intern that the boss likes it when you ask lots and lots of questions ... about S&M.
(2DD)

I DARE YOU to assign an intern the task of getting a photocopy of everyone's hand "for identification purposes."
(2D)

I DARE YOU to dare the intern to do any of the Double-Dog Dares in this book.
(D)

I DARE YOU to dare the intern to do any of the Triple-Dog Dares in this book.
(2D)

I DARE YOU to have the intern pick up your dry cleaning.
(D)

I DARE YOU to have the intern try on your dry cleaning.
(2D)

I DARE YOU | to ask an intern if your feet smell bad.
(2D)

I DARE YOU | to contact an intern's college supervisor partway through the intern's length of service and ask why the intern has never shown up to work.
(D)

I DARE YOU | to post in a conspicuous place a chart of previous interns, giving each one a nickname and rating.
(D)

I DARE YOU | to act, when called as a reference for a past intern, as though you are having trouble remembering him or her—then ultimately saying, "Was that the one with the hare lip?"
(D)

AUTHORIZATION

REQUIRED

I DARE YOU to convince a departing intern that there is a company policy insisting that all interns write an honest commentary sheet critiquing each of the key members of the management team. (2D)

I DARE YOU, once the intern's tenure is up, to e-mail the above commentary sheet to everyone in the office. (2D)

I DARE YOU to place a fake application into the intern supervisor's prospects folder. On it should be noted the fictional prospective intern's 1.2 GPA, 3-foot-4-inch height, 220-pound weight, and "additional skills" of plate-spinning, shaving, and synchronized diving. (2DD)

I DARE YOU to ask an intern "What's your name again?" every day for his or her entire tenure.
(2D)

I DARE YOU to tell an intern the same story about your days as an intern at least five times during his or her intern tenure, changing a key detail every time you tell it.
(D)

HR
DARES

The good folks in the Human Resources department have nothing but your best interest in mind.

Er, right.

Actually, they are the people who tend to give you the most paperwork, the people who tell you your insurance premiums have doubled, and the people who are seated in your boss's office when you are called in to get the bad news.

So go ahead: Dare with impunity. Just know there may be repercussions.

I DARE YOU	to ask if the company benefits package includes coverage for indentured servants. (D)
I DARE YOU	to ask if the company benefits package covers foot-binding. (D)
I DARE YOU	to ask how many vasectomies the company benefits package includes. (2D)
I DARE YOU	to walk into the HR office and ask what form you need to change your ethnicity to "Eskimo." (D)
I DARE YOU	to put "TBA" on the line of any form that asks for your gender. (D)

I DARE YOU | to fill out your next expense report using tally marks instead of numbers.
(D)

I DARE YOU | to ask three questions in the same day to about medical marijuana.
(D)

I DARE YOU | to tell your HR person that you aren't happy with the office curtains.
(D)

I DARE YOU | to formally request that you have approval of all future hires.
(2D)

I DARE YOU | to send a memo to HR strongly suggesting they consider your teenage-dropout cousin for the next opening in management.
(D)

I DARE YOU	to ask your HR person to take your temperature. (2D)
I DARE YOU	to ask your HR person to put a Band-Aid on your ouchie. (D)
I DARE YOU	to ask your HR person if an erection that last more than four hours is a reason to claim a sick day. (2DD)
I DARE YOU	to ask your HR person, "What's insurance?" (D)
I DARE YOU	to ask your HR person if you can see a co-worker's medical file, telling him or her that you are only using it for material for an upcoming roast. (D)

| **I DARE YOU** | to call in sick when you aren't.
 (D) |

| **I DARE YOU** | to call in for a family funeral when there hasn't been one.
 (2D) |

| **I DARE YOU** | to bring a note from your real doctor explaining your absence, and give it to your HR person.
 (D) |

| **I DARE YOU** | to bring a note from Dr. Doolittle explaining your absence, and give it to your HR person.
 (2D) |

| **I DARE YOU** | to bring a note from your Mom explaining your absence, and give it to your HR person.
 (2D |

PRIVATE

OFFICE-SUPPLY ORDER DARES

A highlight of any office darer's month is office-supply ordering day. Usually some office lackey is responsible for taking these orders, and some are careful about what is ordered by whom. Some, however, are not. And if you are blessed to be in such an office, another window of office daring opens up. So when the Staples or Office Depot or other office-supply catalog makes the rounds, consider these dares.

Note that the dare value of these depends on the business conducted by your office, and on the dare-ee's job description. Adjust the ratings accordingly.

I DARE YOU | to order a paper cutter.
(D)

I DARE YOU | to order a portable flip-chart easel.
(D)

I DARE YOU | to order a space heater.
(D)

I DARE YOU | to order a gross of gel pens.
(D)

I DARE YOU | to order a dolly.
(D)

I DARE YOU | to custom-order chocolates bearing the company's logo—misspelled.
(2D)

I DARE YOU | to order a leather chair.
(2D)

I DARE YOU | to order an electronic label-maker.
(D)

I DARE YOU | to order an embosser.
(D)

I DARE YOU | to order number 6 pencils.
(D)

I DARE YOU | to order a carton of sidewalk chalk.
(D)

I DARE YOU | to order poetry magnets.
(D)

SENSITIVE
INFORMATION

CONFIDENTIAL

I DARE YOU	to order a blood-pressure monitor. (D)
I DARE YOU	to order a height and weight scale. (2D)
I DARE YOU	to order a depository safe. (D)
I DARE YOU	to order a portable GPS. (2D)
I DARE YOU	to order an adjustable-height projection stand. (D)
I DARE YOU	to order a fold-n-go work station. (2D)

| **I DARE YOU** | to order a dozen halogen flood lamps. (2D) |

| **I DARE YOU** | to order color-coded rubber bands. (D) |

| **I DARE YOU** | to order a T-square. (D) |

| **I DARE YOU** | to order adhesive bubble wrap. (D) |

| **I DARE YOU** | to order cohesive bubble wrap. (D) |

| **I DARE YOU** | to order a lead x-ray apron. (2D) |

I DARE YOU to order a gross of X-Acto knives.
(2D)

I DARE YOU to order a gross of children's scissors.
(2D)

I DARE YOU to order a laminated map of Antarctica.
(D)

I DARE YOU to order your own bar-code scanner.
(D)

I DARE YOU to order cotton balls.
(D)

I DARE YOU to order a set of basic math flash-cards.
(D)

I DARE YOU | to order a manual typewriter.
(2D)

I DARE YOU | to order a dot-matrix printer.
(2D)

I DARE YOU | to order 100 cubic feet of packing peanuts.
(2D)

FURTHER

I DARE YOU | to eat a bag of packing peanuts.
(2DD)

I DARE YOU | to order tongue depressors.
(D)

I DARE YOU | to order exam-table paper.
(2D)

I DARE YOU to order biohazard waste bags.

(2D)

I DARE YOU to order a 3-x-5-foot American flag.

(D)

APPEARANCE
DARES

Whether you shop at Goodwill or Brooks Brothers, how you present yourself in the office can be as important as what you do work-wise. Many a well-dressed lackey has been promoted over a schlumpy hard worker. In short, it's difficult to succeed in most businesses without really trying to look the part.

Why am I telling you this? Because it follows that, when you dare someone to alter his or her façade, lots of things can happen. And that unknown reaction is half the fun of daring. So consider putting someone up to one of the following challenges. And make sure to have some sort of camera handy. You'll want to post the results somewhere prominent. After all, isn't this why YouTube was created?

I DARE YOU | to wear a kilt to work.
(D)

I DARE YOU | to wear a children's tattoo on your face.
(D)

I DARE YOU | to wear a shirt with the tags still on.
(D)

I DARE YOU | to wear mismatched shoes.
(D)

I DARE YOU | to wear mismatched shoes that are
different colors.
(2D)

I DARE YOU | to wear a pair of white gloves to work.
(D)

I DARE YOU to wear one white glove to work.
(D)

I DARE YOU to wear a fencing mask to work.
(D)

AND, WHEN ASKED ABOUT IT,

I DARE YOU to say that it's a medical thing.
(D)

I DARE YOU to wear an ascot to the next office party.
(D)

I DARE YOU to wear more than one watch to work.
(D)

I DARE YOU to wear binoculars for a full day at work.
(D)

I DARE YOU	to use those binoculars to obviously spy through the windows on the neighboring office building. **(2D)**

I DARE YOU	to file a report based on what you see in the neighboring office building through the binoculars that you were dared to wear to work. **(2D)**

I DARE YOU	to shave only half your face (for hairy folks only). **(2D)**

I DARE YOU	to wear three Band-Aids on your face all day, claiming a shaving mishap. **(D)**

I DARE YOU	to have your barber shave your hair into the shape of the company logo. **(2D)**

I DARE YOU to have your barber shave your hair into the shape of a rival company's logo.
(3DD)

I DARE YOU to remove your bra at your desk without removing your top.
(2D; 2DD if you are a man)

I DARE YOU to wear a (non-cycle) helmet to work.
(D)

I DARE YOU to wear a boutonniere or corsage.
(D)

I DARE YOU to leave your shoes untied all day, ignoring anyone who tells you your shoes are untied.
(D)

| **I DARE YOU** | to grow muttonchops.
(2DD) |

| **I DARE YOU** | to keep your umbrella open all the way to your office or cubicle.
(D) |

| **I DARE YOU** | to ask "New shoes?" to everyone you see through the course of a day.
(D) |

| **I DARE YOU** | to wear a codpiece to work.
(2DD) |

TECHIE-ONLY DARES

While I've tried to keep most of this guide general enough to appeal to all workers, there are some dares that require a specialized knowledge. I'm talking about the folks whose job it is to make you feel like an idiot whenever you can't get your essential office equipment to work.

Not that I'm putting them down. I'd be foolish to do that since, well, they are the keepers of that mystical knowledge that somehow miraculously turns the symbols you touch on the keyboard into documents and e-mails. And so, with nothing but respect for the good folks in the IT cave, I offer a special set of dares.

I DARE YOU | to take a screen shot of a Mac desktop and use it as a screen saver on a co-worker's PC (or vice versa).
(2D)

I DARE YOU | to take everyone out of the administrator group.
(2D)

I DARE YOU | to password a screensaver.
(2D)

I DARE YOU | to change the auto-correct on a co-worker's computer so that it misspells common words
(D).

I DARE YOU | to change the auto-correct on a co-worker's computer so that it replaces common words with expletives.
(D)

I DARE YOU to change a co-worker's pointer icon to an hourglass, leading him or her to believe that the computer is trying to complete a task
(D)

I DARE YOU to remove your boss's spam filter.
(2D)

I DARE YOU to divert every third call from a superior to a brothel in Tijuana.
(2D)

I DARE YOU to use five made-up words the next time you have to explain a computer problem to a worker.
(D)

I DARE YOU to collect the computer mouse from as many offices as you can.
(D)

I **DARE YOU**	to change the language setting on a supervisor's computer. (D)
I **DARE YOU**	to sprinkle a small amount of soil between the keys of an old keyboard, follow it with some grass seed, dampen the mixture, and leave the keyboard outside, watering it regularly. Then, when you've got some growth, swap out the keyboard with that of a co-worker. (2DD)
I **DARE YOU**	to doctor someone's mouse to reverse the functions of the left and right buttons. (D)
I **DARE YOU**	to perform a database upgrade that locks the CEO out of his computer. (2D)

I DARE YOU	to replace a co-worker's wallpaper with wallpaper of a log-in box thus causing confusion. **(D)**

I DARE YOU	to replace the rah-rah corporate video at the annual company meeting with scenes from *The Facts of Life*. **(2DD)**

I DARE YOU	to replace the rah-rah corporate video at the annual company meeting with a montage of scenes of a co-worker's wedding. **(2DD)**

I DARE YOU	to replace the rah-rah corporate video at the annual company meeting with a webcam video of your boss eating a tuna salad sandwich. **(2DD)**

| **I DARE YOU** | to post your in-house training video on YouTube. **(2D)** |

| **I DARE YOU** | to create job-search files for key management staff on Monster.com. **(2DD)** |

| **I DARE YOU** | to spend a day trying to invent a new smiley. **(D)** |

| **I DARE YOU** | to rearrange the keys on a victim's keyboard to spell out a rude comment about a member of his or her family. **(2D)** |

| **I DARE YOU** | to recreate your office in Second Life, people it with every one of your co-workers, and make everyone do your bidding. **(2D)** |

BIG BOSS DARES

I n other sections, I've offered dares involving your boss. But there's plenty more where those came from. Hence this section devoted to those above you. Feel free to adjust them to any supervisor, of course. Just keep in mind that if you are gutsy enough to switch out "boss" with "CEO" or "owner," you get an automatic dare upgrade to the next-higher dare level—turning, for example, a double dare into a double-dog dare.

With that in mind—and with your employment future at stake—here are some Big Boss Dares.

I DARE YOU to tell the boss that his or her spouse "really looks hot" in the photo on his or her desk.
(**2D** if you are of the opposite sex of the spouse; **2DD** if you are of the same sex as the spouse.)

I DARE YOU to, in the middle of a one-on-one meeting, rearrange the objects on your boss's desk.
(**2D**)

I DARE YOU, to, in the middle of a one-on-one meeting with your boss, blow a very large chewing-gum bubble.
(**2DD**)

I DARE YOU to present your boss with a petition requesting Arbor Day off.
(**D**)

| I DARE YOU | to ask your boss if he or she minds if you sit in his or her chair. (2D) |

| I DARE YOU | to mispronounce the boss's name twice in a day. (2D) |

| I DARE YOU | to ask the boss if he's got any McDonald's coupons. (D) |

| I DARE YOU | to try to borrow money from the boss. (2DD) |

| I DARE YOU | to insult the boss's alma mater ... within hearing distance, of course. (2D) |

I DARE YOU | to tell the boss that he looks like he could use a little more fiber.
(2D)

I DARE YOU | to break wind while sitting on the boss's chair.
(2D)

I DARE YOU | to break wind while sitting on the boss's lap.
(3DD)

I DARE YOU | to submit a list of jokes to your boss with the suggestion that he or she "work them into the next meeting."
(D)

I DARE YOU | to plant a bra or jockstrap in your boss's desk drawer.
(2DD)

IF YOUR BOSS IS MALE AND WEARING A TIE,

I DARE YOU | to say, "Yeah, I know how it feels when your kids buy you a tie and you feel like you have to wear it."
(2D)

I DARE YOU | to do some research and find out your boss's college GPA.
(2D)

SPECIAL DAYS AT WORK DARES

While it sometimes may feel that every day in the office is the same—that life consists of two kinds of days, horrible workdays and blissful weekend days—the reality is that occasionally a special day comes along that is different from the rest. Some of these days require special office activities and attention, situations ripe for dares. Others require a more subtle approach.

Whichever the case, here are some special dares to make those special days even more memorable.

ARBOR DAY DARE

I DARE YOU | to celebrate Arbor Day by planting a seed in the oldest food item in the refrigerator.
(D)

CHRISTMAS DARES

I DARE YOU | to "accidentally" call your boss "Ebenezer" at least once a week throughout the month of December.
(2D)

I DARE YOU | to replace each of your co-worker's names in the draw-a-name-from-a-hat office gift-exchange with slips of paper all bearing the same name—preferably that of the least-noticed person in your office.
(2DD)

I DARE YOU | to actually wear a lampshade on your head at the holiday party.
(2D)

I DARE YOU to wear a burka to the holiday party.
(2DD)

I DARE YOU to carry around mistletoe and threaten everyone of the opposite sex with its use.
(2D)

I DARE YOU to hire an "escort" to bring as a guest to the next office holiday party.
(2DD)

I DARE YOU to throw a snowball at your boss right before the office holiday party.
(2DD; 3DD if you live in a climate where it doesn't snow at all)

NEW YEAR'S EVE DARES

I DARE YOU, on the last workday before New Year's Eve, to say "See you next year" to everyone in the office at least twice.
(D)

I DARE YOU to take every opportunity on the day you get back after New Year's Eve, to make a big deal about mistakenly writing the previous year on checks, letters, etc.
(D)

ANNIVERSARY DATE DARE

I DARE YOU to send yourself a large bouquet of flowers, from the boss, on your employment anniversary date.
(D)

BOSS'S BIRTHDAY DARE

I DARE YOU to hire a singing-telegram delivery person—or, if you can't book one, have your friend act as a singing-telegram delivery person—to serenade your boss with "Whistle While You Work."
(2D)

I DARE YOU to bring in a cake with the boss's name misspelled.
(D)

I DARE YOU | to bring in a cake for your boss with the wrong name on it.
(2DD)

YOUR BIRTHDAY DARES

IF YOU HAVE ONE OF THOSE OFFICES WHERE EVERYONE'S BIRTHDAY IS CELEBRATED,

I DARE YOU | to refuse to blow out the candles on your birthday cake.
(DD)

HALLOWEEN DARES

I DARE YOU | to come to work dressed as your boss.
(2DD)

I DARE YOU | to eat, on the first work day after Halloween, in front of co-workers and without acknowledging the strangeness of it, a lunch consisting of nothing but candy.
(D)

I DARE YOU | to bring to the office a pumpkin carved to resemble your boss.
(2D)

ST. PATRICK'S DAY DARES

I DARE YOU | to say to co-workers, after lunch, "You've been drinking, haven't you?"
(2D)

I DARE YOU | to arrive at the office drunk
(3D).

I DARE YOU | to challenge a supervisor to a game of quarters.
(2DD)

I DARE YOU | to dye the water-cooler water green.
(D)

I DARE YOU | to sing "Danny Boy" to anyone in the office named Daniel or Dan.
(2D)

MARTIN LUTHER KING'S BIRTHDAY DARE

I DARE YOU | to spend the next day (or that day, if you are working it) telling people about the dreams you had.
(D)

ASH WEDNESDAY DARE

I DARE YOU | to come to work with ashes covering at least 30 percent of your face.
(3D)

EARTH DAY DARES

I DARE YOU | to root through other people's trash cans for recyclable materials.
(D)

SENSITIVE MATERIALS

I DARE YOU | to string together chains of cans from the recycling bin and tie them to the back of a co-workers car.
(2D)

PURIM DARE

I DARE YOU | to shout "*Booooooo*" any time your boss's name is mentioned. (Ask a rabbi to explain this one to you.)
(2D)

PRESIDENTS DAY DARE

I DARE YOU | to wear a powdered wig to work.
(2D)

VALENTINE'S DAY DARE

I DARE YOU | to pick a random co-worker and send him or her a bouquet of flowers from "Chet, with my deepest love."
(D)

I DARE YOU | to bite into each piece in a box of chocolates and then put them in the break room to share.
(2D)

I DARE YOU | to post a giant heart, anywhere visible in the office, with your initials + the name of your company.
(2D)

ST. CRISPIN'S DAY DARES
(Oct. 25, for those of you who were not English or History majors)

I DARE YOU | to stand on your chair and recite the St. Crispin's Day speech from Williams Shakespeare's *Henry V* in its entirety ("We few, we happy few, we band of brothers; ...").
(2DD; **3DD** if you are carrying a sword when you do it)

EASTER DARES

I DARE YOU | to hide uncooked eggs around the office.
(2DD)

I DARE YOU | to give someone a chocolate bunny with the ears already bitten off.
(2D)

THANKSGIVING DARES

I DARE YOU | to eat, on the Monday after Thanksgiving weekend, in front of co-workers and without acknowledging the strangeness of it, a lunch consisting of nothing but cranberry sauce.
(D)

I DARE YOU | to eat, on the Monday after Thanksgiving weekend, in front of co-workers and without acknowledging the strangeness of it, a lunch consisting of nothing but a bowl of gravy.
(D)

APRIL FOOL'S DAY DARE

I DARE YOU to do nothing out of the ordinary, but look very suspicious.
(D)

CLEARANCE REQUIRED

AUTHORIZED

DATE_____ SECTION_____

BOSS-TO-BOSS DARES

This section assumes you are in charge of your office. And you know someone who is the head honcho at a different office. Who's to say you still can't dare?

While it's bad form for someone to offer up a dare to someone lower on the food chain (for then it would be an order rather than a dare), it's perfectly OK for one boss to dare another boss. Of course, given that in most cases a boss isn't taking much risk in following through on a dare, you won't find any double or triple dares here.

Nonetheless, Mr. Head Honcho, here are some ideas.

| I DARE YOU | to declare Friday "Orange and Mauve Day."
 (D) |

| I DARE YOU | to use the phrase "outside the box" in every conversation you have in an entire day.
 (D) |

| I DARE YOU | to post a reminder sheet in your office listing the "Last hired."
 (D) |

| I DARE YOU | to raise everyone's salary by three cents, explaining that it will actually help over in accounting.
 (D) |

| I DARE YOU | to send an interoffice envelope to yourself containing nothing but a cantaloupe.
 (2D) |

I DARE YOU | to have an interoffice contest in which the winner wins a pair of tickets to your toddler's birthday party.
(D)

I DARE YOU | to declare one of your underlings "Employee of the Hour."
(D)

I DARE YOU | to requisition an abacus for the accounting department.
(D)

I DARE YOU | to hire a caricaturist to spend an afternoon drawing your staff.
(D)

FURTHER

I DARE YOU | to charge your staff for the caricaturist's drawings.
(D)

EVEN FURTHER

I DARE YOU	to sign those drawings and hang them in your office. **(D)**

I DARE YOU	to bring into the office a person who makes animal balloons, telling everyone that he is your brother-in-law, and dropping hints that you are considering hiring him. **(D)**

I DARE YOU	to page a staffer, have him come into your office, ask him to explain the electoral college to you, thank him, and send him back to his cubicle. **(D)**

I DARE YOU	to include a coupon in everyone's next paycheck offering 40 cents off their next purchase of Windex. **(D)**

I DARE YOU | to call your cell phone from your office phone and have a half-hour conversation with yourself.
(D)

I DARE YOU | to rationalize putting a foosball table in your office.
(D)

I DARE YOU | to start each morning for a week by playing "We Are Family" over the office loudspeaker.
(D)

NEXT
JOB
DARES

There is a very good chance that if you've made any of these dares (or were yourself dared), you no longer have a job.

First let me offer you my condolences. (And let me remind you that at the beginning of this book, I explicitly asked you not to blame the author or publisher for the fallout from any of these dares. Remember? Go back and check if you need to.)

Once you've accepted that you've got to move on, think of this as not just another phase in your life, but also the opportunity for a new set of dares. Consider the following.

NEXT JOB DARES | 183

I DARE YOU to include on your resume mention of the American Legion essay contest you won in middle school.
(2D)

I DARE YOU to include on your resume that you are president of a *Gossip Girl* fan club.
(2D)

I DARE YOU to include on your resume the number of times you saw *Star Wars*.
(D)

I DARE YOU to include with your resume a photo of yourself in Renaissance garb.
(D)

I DARE YOU to list a prison cell as your home address on your resume.
(2DD)

I DARE YOU | to print your resume on scented and/or flowered paper.
(2DD)

I DARE YOU | to give your e-mail address on your resume as **Ilovetosnuggle@hugs.com**.
(2DD)

I DARE YOU | to include under "References" on your resume, "Just don't talk to my ex."
(D)

I DARE YOU | to call the just-met receptionist at your potential new company "Babe."
(2D, assuming you are a man and she is a woman.)

I DARE YOU | to call the just-met receptionist at your potential new company "Babe."
(2D, assuming you are a woman and he is a man.)

I DARE YOU	to call the just-met receptionist at your potential new company "Babe." (**2D**, assuming you are a woman and she is a woman.)

I DARE YOU	to call the just-met receptionist at your potential new company "Babe." (**2DD**, assuming you are a man and he is a man.)

I DARE YOU	to, before sitting down in your potential boss's office for an interviewer, spray disinfectant on your chair. (**2DD**)

I DARE YOU	to, after shaking your potential boss's hand, use a hand sanitizer on yours. (**2DD**)

I DARE YOU to comment on your prospective new boss's office with the phrase, "I like a guy with a sense of kitsch."
(2D)

I DARE YOU to answer your next job interviewer's "Why should we hire you?" question by saying, "You sure ask a lot of questions."
(D)

I DARE YOU to answer your next job interviewer's "Why should we hire you?" question by saying, "Who wants to know?"
(2DD)

I DARE YOU to answer your next job interviewer's "Why should we hire you?" question by saying, "Because I have photos that you don't want me to share."
(3D)

I DARE YOU to take out a Pez dispenser during your next job interview and offer a candy to the interviewer.
(D)

I DARE YOU to ask during your next job interview if Viagra is covered by the company's prescription health plan.
(2D)

I DARE YOU to make a cell-phone call in the middle of your next job interview.
(2D)

I DARE YOU to, when taking a tour of the workplace of your next potential job, trip over an imaginary object.
(D)

I DARE YOU to, when taking a tour of the workplace of your next potential job, walk ahead of your interviewer and blaze your own trail.

(2D)

I DARE YOU to, after your next job interview, send flowers to the interviewer with a note saying, "Plenty more where these came from."

(2D)

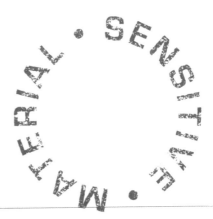

OFFICE
DARES
DARES

Yes, this book is meant to inspire you, bring some laughs, and open your mind to how you can make the workday a little less tedious. The proper use of this book is simple: Find a dare you like ... dare someone ... then watch the fallout.

But if you've learned anything from reading this far, it's that there's always a new and interesting way to dare. Consider these *Office Dares* dares.

I DARE YOU | to buy this book for everyone in your office. And then send them each an invoice for it.
(2DD)

I DARE YOU | to suggest this book for your book club.
(D)

IF YOU RECEIVED THIS BOOK AS A GIFT,

I DARE YOU | to attempt to return it to your local bookstore for cash.
(D)

I DARE YOU | to tear out every page and staple or tape each one up somewhere in the office.
(2D)

I DARE YOU | to organize a protest against any bookseller selling this book.
(2D)

I DARE YOU	to look for hidden messages in this book. **(D)**
I DARE YOU	to go to your favorite on-line bookseller and post a rave review, using the word "ubiquitous" somewhere in the text so that I know it came from someone accepting this dare. **(2D)**
I DARE YOU	to nuke this book in the office microwave. **(D)**
I DARE YOU	to leave this book for a week in the office freezer. **(D)**

HAND DELIVER ONLY

I DARE YOU to e-mail a list of these dares (giving full credit to the book, of course) to everyone on your e-mail list.
(2D)

I DARE YOU to invite author Lou Harry to speak at your next annual meeting.
(2DD)

I DARE YOU to invite author Lou Harry to speak at your next annual meeting ... and attach a generous per diem and luxury accommodations along with the necessary travel expenses.
(3DD)

YOUR VERY OWN OFFICE DARES

While there are hundreds of office dares included in this book, there are surely thousands more thought of by others—or yet to be thought of. That's where you come in. No doubt these have gotten your mind working. You have come up with some dares you've already initiated, or wish you had the spine to initiate.

Either way, I'd love to hear from you. Post dares you've made—or dares you haven't had the heart to make—at **www.officedares.com**. Posted dares become the property of Cider Mill Press, publishers of this book, but that's OK. You weren't going to publish them elsewhere, right? Here, at least, we'll give you credit if we use them in a future edition.

Not sure if you want to post one online? Maybe this will help:

I DARE YOU	to post your own dare at **www.officedares.com**.

Or maybe this:

I DOUBLE-DARE YOU	to post something there. And consider it a triple dare if you post it from your boss's computer.